5/97

Diabetes

Expert Review by
Jerrold S. Olshan, M.D.

Crestwood House
Parsippany, New Jersey

CAROL
McCORMICK
SEMPLE

HEALTH ■ WATCH

Dedicated to the memory of my grandfather, Euletario DiFolco, and my uncle, Domenic DiFolco

Acknowledgments
With thanks to:
████ Jerrold S. Olshan, M.D., Director, Division of Pediatric and Adolescent Endocrinology/Diabetes, Maine Medical Center, for his advice and review of this book.
████ Alysha Comeau and her family for their willingness to share their story.

Photo Credits
Cover: *l.* Carl D. Walsh. *m.* Michael Rosenfeld/Tony Stone Images. *r.* Courtesy Eli Lilly Co.
Graphics Courtesy, Eli Lilly Co.: 13, 14, 15, 20, 21. Courtesy, Comeau family: 4. Courtesy, Lifescan, A Johnson & Johnson company: 31. Courtesy, Eli Lilly Co.: 8 *t.*, 23, 40. Courtesy, National Institutes of Health: 19. © St. Bartholomew's Hospital/Science Photo Library/ Photo Researchers, Inc.: 29. Yoav Levy/Phototake NYC: 22. SuperStock: 34. Carl D. Walsh: 8 *b.*, 9, 33, 35.

Cover and book design by Lisa Ann Arcuri

 Published by Crestwood House,
A Division of Simon & Schuster,
299 Jefferson Road, Parsippany, NJ 07054

First Edition
Printed in the United States of America
10 9 8 7 6 5 4 3 2 1

Library of Congress Cataloging-in-Publication Data

Semple, Carol McCormick
    Diabetes / by Carol McCormick Semple.
        p. cm. — (HealthWatch)
    Includes bibliographical references and index.
    ISBN 0-89686-860-5
    1. Diabetes—Juvenile literature. [1. Diabetes.
    2. Diseases.]
I. Title. II. Series.
RC660.5.S45   1996
616.4'62—dc20   94-26501

Summary: Discusses the two types of diabetes, including treatment, the complications from the disease, and research related to treatment and a possible cure.

Contents

Diabetic Alysha Comeau enjoys cross-country skiing on a sunny winter day in Maine.

Chapter 1

Meet Alysha

Alysha Comeau loves to race down-hill on skis. In the summer she spends much of her time in the water, swimming or water skiing. She takes ballet classes and has danced in *The Nutcracker* ballet.

Alysha also has **diabetes mellitus**, often called just diabetes. She must have two injections with a needle every day. Her mother carefully keeps track to make sure Alysha eats the right foods each day. Alysha's fingers have been pricked so many times to test her blood that their skin is marked and tough.

Diabetes is a disease that prevents the body from using food properly. In one type of diabetes—the type Alysha has—the body has stopped making a substance it needs. The substance is called **insulin**. Alysha gets her insulin in the shots she takes each day.

Alysha, who is nine, has blond hair and a bright face. She lives in Naples, Maine, with her parents; her five-year-old sister, Catherine; a guinea pig; and a cat. She has a calm manner and doesn't mind talking about diabetes.

"The thing I don't want to do that I have to do is [take] the shots," Alysha says.

Alysha has had diabetes since she was five. Her mother, Beth Comeau, brought her to a doctor one summer day when she noticed Alysha had to keep using the bathroom. Alysha had been getting up several times in the night to urinate.

Doctors gave Alysha a simple blood test that took only a few minutes. It showed that Alysha had about seven times more sugar in her blood than normal. Her **blood sugar** was at a level where some people would be in danger of going into a **coma,** which is like a deep sleep. Most children with diabetes, though, don't go into a coma. Alysha's mother immediately took her to the hospital on the doctor's orders.

"She didn't look sick. She hadn't lost weight. We caught it early," Beth Comeau says.

Living with Diabetes

Alysha and her mother spent two days at the hospital. Shots of insulin got the amount of sugar in Alysha's blood back to normal. Without daily shots, the amount of sugar would rise again. At the hospital Alysha and her mother learned how to measure and give the shots and how to administer the blood sugar test. Mrs. Comeau and Alysha's father, Fern, also had to learn what kind of foods Alysha could eat.

Alysha and her family were afraid at first. "I felt like I had a baby again," Mrs. Comeau recalls.

At first Mrs. Comeau felt overwhelmed when she went grocery shopping. Alysha must have foods that are low in sugar and fat. "You think peanut butter and crackers is a good snack, but it turns out it has a lot of sugar in it," Mrs. Comeau says. Managing Alysha's diet has become easier as the family learns more about foods.

Alysha started kindergarten that fall. One of her classmates was afraid she would catch diabetes from Alysha. But, as the teacher explained, diabetes is not a disease you can catch from another person. "It didn't make me feel good," Alysha says, recalling her classmate's reaction. "But now everyone is fine about it."

Alysha is in the fourth grade now. She is not shy about taking her insulin shots or

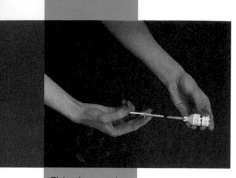

This shows the proper way to draw insulin from the bottle into a syringe.

doing her blood tests when her friends are there. Alysha has been able to prepare and give herself her own shots since she was seven. Her mother usually gives them, though. Her mother also prepares the insulin to make sure it is the right amount. One of Alysha's friends likes to help with the shot. Sometimes, just out of curiosity, a friend will do a fingertip blood test on herself when Alysha does.

Alysha takes her insulin twice a day at home. She must test her blood about four

Alysha Comeau prepares to give herself a shot of insulin in her leg.

times a day and before she exercises. Blood tests are important because people with diabetes can have a reaction if their insulin, food, and exercise don't balance. An insulin shot or exercise will cause blood sugar to go down. If the amount of sugar in Alysha's blood is too low, she may get shaky and not know where she is. She may even pass out. This is called an insulin reaction. If Alysha's blood sugar is too low, she needs to eat sugar quickly. It's the one time a person with diabetes needs to eat something sweet.

Alysha had her first insulin reaction the week after she came home from the hospital. Alysha takes good care of herself, so she hasn't had many bad reactions. Her mother has learned that the quickest way to stop a bad reaction is to put maple syrup under Alysha's tongue. That gives her the sugar she needs immediately.

Mrs. Comeau was surprised to learn that Alysha's teachers had never had a diabetic student before. The Comeau family has had to teach them about the disease.

At school, if Alysha feels a reaction beginning, she gets a drink of orange

Diabetic Alysha Comeau takes a blood sample from her finger to check her blood sugar levels.

juice. Orange juice contains a lot of sugar and it gets into her system quickly. Her teacher keeps a kit handy in case of a reaction. It contains juice, peanut butter crackers, and hard candy.

Alysha has learned to recognize when she should quickly drink orange juice. "My stomach sort of feels weird and I sort of feel weak," she says.

The Comeaus try to be prepared at all times. When Alysha skis, she carries a candy bar in her jacket. She can eat the candy for fast sugar if she feels shaky or if she can't eat her meal on time.

Alysha hasn't had to make any more trips to the hospital, but she sees her family doctor regularly. In most cases it is important to see a specially trained team to deal with diabetes. Patients check in with the team regularly to be sure that their diabetes is under control.

Mrs. Comeau says the family's attitude has been the key to coping with the disease. Alysha accepts her diabetes but doesn't make a big deal out of it. She sticks to her diet. Mrs. Comeau lets her daughter be a kid. Once in a while, she lets Alysha have a piece of candy. She makes up for it somewhere else in her diet or in the amount of her insulin shot.

"She never sneaks food," her mother says. "If someone gave her a Hershey's kiss as a reward, she would bring it home and say, 'Can I eat this?'"

On Halloween, Alysha loves to go trick or treating even though she can't eat much of what she collects. She enjoys getting dressed up in a costume and going out anyway. Her mother says it helps that Alysha never liked to eat sweets. She didn't eat sugary cereals before she became diabetic, so she never had to cut them out of her diet.

The most difficult times for Alysha are when she gets a cold or flu. Sickness puts stress on the body and leads to higher blood-sugar levels. Alysha's blood sugar is high just before she gets sick. Sickness makes it harder to keep the blood sugar even.

People with diabetes can get help from talking with others who have the disease. Some go to support groups to share feelings and information about diabetes.

When the Comeaus were at the hospital, they met a nurse whose daughter is diabetic, and they learned much from their new friends. A doctor they know keeps them up to date on research. The family hopes that new discoveries will make it easier for Alysha to get the insulin she needs.

Alysha and her family have taken charge of Alysha's diabetes rather than let it take charge of her. She plans to become a doctor when she grows up.

"We're lucky that she's in such good control," Mrs. Comeau says.

Chapter 2

What Is Diabetes?

Diabetes mellitus prevents the body's cells from using food properly. Our bodies turn many of the foods we eat into sugar. This sugar, called **glucose**, gives us energy and makes us grow. Instead of using the sugar, a person with diabetes passes it out of the body in his or her urine. The word *diabetes* comes from the Greek word meaning "to cross over or pass through." *Mellitus* comes from the Latin word meaning "honey."

There are two kinds of diabetes mellitus: Type I and Type II. They have different causes, but they are similar in that they both stem from problems with insulin.

Insulin is a **hormone**. A hormone is a chemical that brings a message from one part of the body to another. The message tells the body what to do. Our bodies make many hormones to do special jobs.

The **pancreas** makes insulin. The pancreas is a long, oddly shaped gland that lies behind the stomach. Insulin lets our bodies use the food we eat. We would die without insulin.

Some people compare insulin to a key that unlocks the body's cells. Once they are unlocked, sugar can get in to feed these cells. Without insulin, sugar builds up in the blood instead of entering the cells. That means your whole body—heart, brain, muscles—isn't getting food. It is always dangerous to have a lot of sugar in your blood.

Stomach

Pancreas

This graphic shows the location of the pancreas in the body.

Type I Diabetes

Diabetes starts in some people when their pancreas stops making insulin or makes only a small amount. This kind of diabetes is called Type I. It is also called insulin-dependent diabetes. It usually starts in children or in young adults, but it can begin at any age. Because it often starts when people are young, Type I used to be

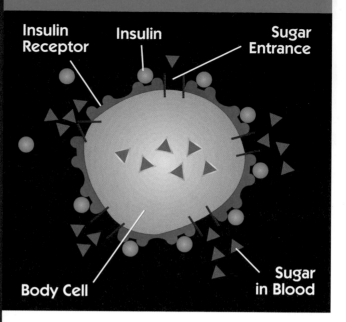

This shows the mechanism that controls the entrance of sugar into a cell. When there is enough insulin in the blood to fill the insulin receptors, the receptors open and the sugar enters the cell. This causes the level of sugar in the blood to drop.

Insulin Receptor

Insulin

Sugar Entrance

Body Cell

Sugar in Blood

called juvenile-onset diabetes (*onset* means "beginning"). A person with Type I diabetes must have shots of insulin every day.

When Type I diabetes starts, a person may lose weight. He or she may constantly feel hungry and thirsty and may eat lots of food. But the sugar stays in the blood; it can't get past the locked doors to the rest of the body's cells. So even though the person is eating, the body isn't being fed.

At first, people with Type I diabetes feel weak and tired. Even after a good night's sleep they may feel the way you do at the end of a busy day when you haven't eaten for many hours. They will probably get grumpy. They may feel sick and vomit. They will urinate more often as their bod-

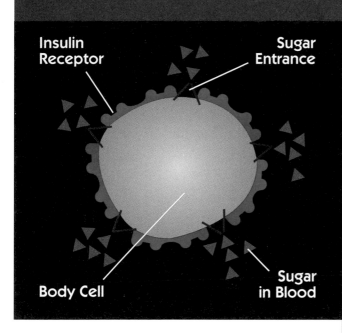

Insulin Receptor

Sugar Entrance

Body Cell

Sugar in Blood

When there is not enough insulin in the blood to fill the insulin receptors, the receptors stay closed. Because sugar cannot enter the cell, sugar levels in the blood rise.

ies pass sugar. They may accidentally wet the bed at night. Such accidents may be confusing and embarrassing.

You can't tell whether a person has diabetes by looking at him or her. A doctor can tell when a person has Type I diabetes by doing a blood test. If sugar is trapped in the blood, then the test will show a level higher than normal. About 1 million Americans have Type I diabetes. Many of them are children and teenagers.

Scientists don't know exactly what causes Type I diabetes, but they are learning more about it all the time. Doctors have found that the disease runs in families. But people don't inherit diabetes from their parents in the same way they inherit their eye color. Scientists have linked Type I diabetes to a common virus. For some reason, the virus may damage the pancreas in some people.

Researchers have also learned that Type I diabetes is an **autoimmune** disease. The immune system is supposed to attack harmful germs in the body. When someone has an autoimmune disease, the signals get mixed up. When that happens, the body's immune system attacks a part of the body. In the case of Type I diabetes, the body destroys the cells in the pancreas that produce insulin. Studies are being done to find out why the body makes this mistake.

Type II Diabetes

Type II diabetes usually starts when a person is older than 40, but it can start at any age. Type II diabetes is different from Type I in some important ways.

The pancreas of a person with Type II diabetes makes insulin. In some cases it may not make all that the body needs. More often, the pancreas is making plenty of insulin, but for some reason the body cannot use it. The body has the insulin key but the door still won't open. This is one big difference between Type I and Type II diabetes.

People with Type II diabetes usually do not have to have insulin shots. Often they can control the disease with pills or diet. This type of diabetes used to be called maturity-onset diabetes because it usually affects adults. It is now usually called noninsulin-dependent diabetes.

Type II diabetes develops slowly. Some people don't even know they have it. Most people who get Type II diabetes are overweight.

Just as in Type I, people with Type II diabetes may begin to lose weight because their cells aren't being fed. They feel hungry and thirsty all the time. They also have to urinate more often. Their vision may get blurry. They may discover that cuts don't heal fast. Sometimes their hands and feet feel tingly. And they may keep getting infections that won't go away. A doctor can tell whether a person has Type II diabetes by doing a blood test.

More people have Type II diabetes than Type I. About 13 million Americans have Type II diabetes.

Doctors are still trying to discover what causes Type II diabetes. Scientists know that Type II diabetes is more hereditary than Type I. They also know that being seriously overweight can trigger Type II diabetes. But it is not an autoimmune disease. And scientists haven't linked it to any virus.

More people have been getting diabetes each year in the United States. Scientists think that is because there are more older people in our country now. They also believe it is because more people are overweight.

Chapter 3

Complications from Diabetes

iabetes is a dangerous disease because it causes other health problems. Scientists suspect that when blood-sugar levels go way up and way down, these changes cause damage to the blood vessels. But they don't know why the damage occurs. Damage to the blood vessels can in turn damage the eyes, the kidneys, and the nerves. Diabetes also can lead to problems with the large blood vessels that feed the body's organs, especially the heart. All of these problems can happen in people with Type I and Type II diabetes. These problems make diabetes

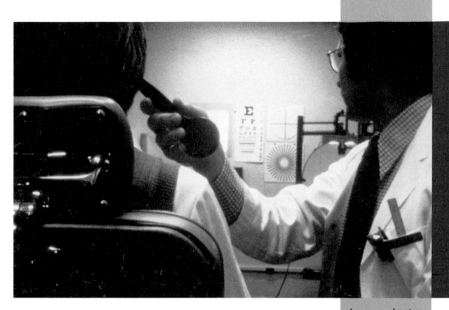

An eye doctor examining a patient. Diabetics must have regular eye exams because the disease causes their vision to deterioriate.

one of the top four causes of death by disease in the United States.

People who have had diabetes for a long time may begin to notice they can't see well. Objects may secm blurry or spotty. This happens when the small blood vessels in the eyes have been damaged. Diabetes is one of the nation's leading causes of blindness. People with diabetes need to have regular eye checkups.

Sometimes diabetes causes damage to the small blood vessels in the **kidneys**. If too many blood vessels are damaged in the kidneys, the kidneys will fail. Every person has two kidneys. They are located below and behind the stomach. The kidneys act as filters for the body. They take wastes out of the blood and remove them from the body in urine. The kidneys of a

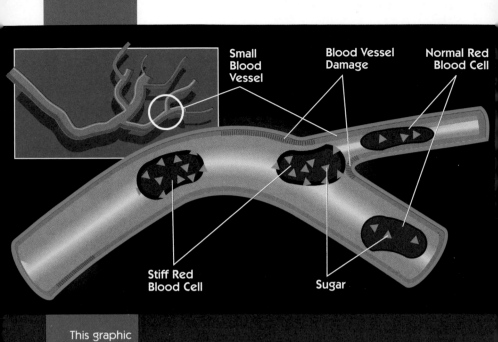

Small Blood Vessel

Blood Vessel Damage

Normal Red Blood Cell

Stiff Red Blood Cell

Sugar

person with diabetes must work extra hard to remove the sugar that isn't being turned into energy. The kidneys are doubly stressed by the extra work and by the blood vessel damage. If a person's kidneys are not working properly, poisons can build up in the body. These poisons will cause death.

People whose kidneys aren't working properly can have the poisons removed by a machine. This process is called **dialysis**. These expensive treatments must be done in a hospital or a special center several times a week. Some people need kidney transplants. Up to half the people with Type I diabetes currently develop kidney disease. Scientists hope that new treatments and drugs will lower that number.

Some people, especially those with Type II diabetes, are at a high risk for changes in the large blood vessels. The lining of the vessels may get thick. This slows down or blocks the flow of blood. When this happens, heart disease can develop or the person can suffer a stroke. People with diabetes are also more likely to develop high blood pressure than other people. For these reasons, the risk of heart attack is high in people with diabetes.

Poor blood flow can also lead to nerve damage. This happens mostly in the hands, legs, and feet. They may feel tingly or hurt, or the person may lose some of

This graphic shows how high blood sugar damages large blood vessels. These damaged areas can trap cholesterol.

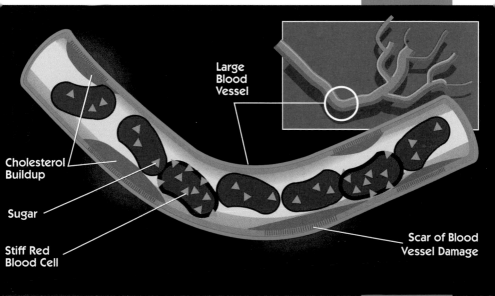

Large Blood Vessel

Cholesterol Buildup

Sugar

Stiff Red Blood Cell

Scar of Blood Vessel Damage

their feeling there. Nerve damage can lead to serious problems. A person may get a cut on the bottom of the foot and not know it. The cut may become infected and not heal. Sometimes the foot must be removed. This makes good foot care important for people with diabetes.

Women with diabetes must be careful to keep the disease under control before they become pregnant and during a pregnancy. If the level of sugar in a woman's blood is not regular, her baby could have birth defects. Mothers with diabetes often have large babies. But a woman with diabetes can have a healthy baby. She must follow her diet. Sometimes she may have to get up in the middle of the night to eat a snack to keep the sugar in her blood as level as possible. She must test her blood and urine often and see her doctor regularly.

A doctor takes the blood pressure of a patient.

Some women get diabetes for the first time when they are pregnant. The disease may stop after the baby is born. These women run a high risk of getting diabetes again when they are older.

All of these problems make diabetes sound scary. People who have just found out they have the disease may feel afraid and sad. They may also feel overwhelmed.

Diabetes is an expensive disease to have. Diabetics must buy insulin or pills, **syringes** to inject the insulin, and blood- and urine-testing equipment. They must see their doctors regularly. Treating the other problems that diabetes causes costs a lot. People in the United States spend an estimated $40 billion each year to treat diabetes and the problems it brings.

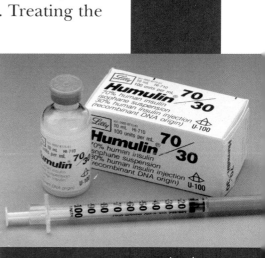

A syringe and bottle of mixed insulin

People who have diabetes today can benefit from much research that has been conducted. One example is an important study done in 1993. It showed that problems were less likely to happen when diabetics kept their blood sugar close to normal. To do this, people with diabetes must test their blood often. They may have to take more insulin shots. They also have to stick to their diets and not "cheat." Usually patients do best when they are also seen monthly by special teams who are experts in diabetes. The teams call the patients on the phone at least once a week to see how they are doing.

Chapter 4

The Miracle of Insulin

Before insulin was discovered in 1921, people with diabetes had no hope of survival. The ancient Egyptians and Greeks could tell that certain people had diabetes because they were thirsty and had to urinate frequently. One first-century writer described the disease as "a melting down of the flesh and limbs into urine." Other ancient doctors discovered that the urine of diabetics tasted sweet. This became the first test for diabetes.

People with Type I diabetes often died within a year after the disease started. Those with Type II often died of the other problems it caused. Doctors learned that the disease was tied to the body's ability to use food. Many doctors believed that certain diets would help their patients.

In the early years of the twentieth century, diabetics were faced with a choice of fad diets. There were the oat cure, the milk diet, the rice cure, and potato therapy. One of the most successful at prolonging life was the "starvation diet." These treatments sound strange today, but doctors at the time tried to use the little knowledge they had. They were hoping to win a battle against a disease that left patients desperate for any relief.

The Search for an Answer

As early as 1889, research showed that diabetes had something to do with the pancreas. Doctors at the time didn't know there was such a thing as insulin, let alone that the pancreas makes it. A few years later another researcher linked diabetes to islands of cells in the pancreas called the **islets of Langerhans**. (They were discovered in 1869 by a German medical student named Paul Langerhans. He had no idea what the mysterious "islands" did.)

Doctors believed that the pancreas made a substance that would provide a clue to diabetes. Many scientists tried to make an extract from the pancreas that would relieve diabetes. They all failed.

Then, in 1920, a young Canadian surgeon had an idea. Dr. Frederick Banting wanted to try an experiment to separate the islet cells from the rest of the pancreas. He hoped to capture the substance the islets make. A professor at the University of Toronto gave him a small lab for his research in the summer of 1921. Banting's assistant was Charles Best, a graduate medical student. Many doctors told Banting and Best that two young researchers could never do what experts had failed to do.

But Banting believed in his idea. He was determined to continue, even when his early results were disappointing.

Banting and Best's months in the lab were full of frustration, arguments, and excitement. Finally they found the substance they were looking for. At first they named it "isletin," after the islets of Langerhans. Its name was later changed to insulin. Their work won them a Nobel Prize in 1923.

"Too Wonderful for Words"

One of the first patients to try insulin was a 15-year-old girl named Elizabeth Hughes. In August 1922 she was 5 feet tall, weighed 45 pounds, and would not have survived the disease much longer. After several weeks of receiving insulin, she began to eat again. She felt better and began to gain weight. She wrote home to her mother, "Oh, it is simply too wonderful for words, this stuff."

Elizabeth Hughes went to college, married a lawyer, had three children, and traveled around the world. She died of a heart attack at the age of 73.

Chapter 5

A Balancing Act: Controlling Diabetes

There is no cure for diabetes. But there is much a person can do to control the disease. By managing diabetes, a person can lead a long, full life.

Some people you know may have diabetes. A teacher, a minister, a teammate, or the girl who sits next to you in class could have diabetes, and you might not know it. Jerry Garcia, the songwriter and guitarist for the Grateful Dead, has diabetes. The actress Mary Tyler Moore does, too. Jim "Catfish" Hunter, who pitched for the Oakland A's and the New York Yankees, has diabetes. So does Wade

Wilson, a quarterback with the New Orleans Saints.

People with diabetes can go to school and participate in activities like anyone else. They can become doctors, engineers, nurses, and computer experts. The Americans with Disabilities Act became law in July 1992. It forbids employers to discriminate against anyone with a disability, including people with diabetes.

The key to living with diabetes is control. People with diabetes must figure out, with their doctors, how much insulin to take, how often to eat, and when to exercise. They must follow this treatment plan every day. They can't take a break from it. They must always think about their illness. This is especially important when planning an activity, a trip, or anything

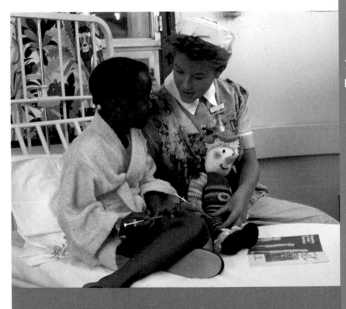

A nurse teaches a young diabetic patient how to give herself insulin injections.

that might change their routine. It takes hard work to manage the illness.

The Right Balance

There is no one plan that works for everyone. The needs of each diabetic are different, and they may change from day to day. People with diabetes learn their own body's needs as they live with the disease. A person's blood sugar will rise after he or she eats. An insulin shot will cause blood sugar to go down. So will exercise. These are the basics that a diabetic must balance each day.

The goal of people with diabetes is to keep their blood sugar as close to normal as possible. They try to avoid highs and lows. A nearly normal blood-sugar level lets a person with diabetes function normally. It also helps prevent some of the problems that make diabetes so dangerous.

Blood testing is an important tool that people with diabetes use in keeping track of their blood sugar. People with both types of the disease must test their blood. They can use the test to decide whether their blood-sugar level should be lower or higher.

The test is done by pricking the finger with a special needle called a lancet. A drop of blood is placed on a test strip. Some people use test strips that change color to show the blood-sugar level. Others use strips that they run through a small meter. The meter

Obtain Sample

Place PENLET® II against side of finger. Press button on side.

Squeeze finger to get a good-sized hanging drop of blood.

gives a digital reading of the person's blood sugar. These tests often must be done several times a day.

A person with Type I diabetes needs insulin shots to survive. Most Type I diabetics inject themselves once or twice daily. They try to do this at the same time each day. There are different kinds of insulin: Some act slowly, some act fast, and some are in between.

Insulin must be given as an injection with a needle or another device that injects it under the skin. It can be injected into the legs, arms, belly, or buttocks. It can't be swallowed because it is a protein, and stomach acids would break it down.

In the past, insulin used by diabetics came from cattle and pigs. Genetic methods now allow scientists to make human insulin in labs. This type of insulin became widely used in the 1980s.

This device uses infrared light and a specially treated paper to measure the level of sugar in a drop of blood.

31

Diet and Exercise

Taking insulin shots is not enough, by itself, to keep good control of Type I diabetes. Eating the right foods in the right amount at the right times is also important. Diabetics must work out a menu plan that is best for them.

In general, people with diabetes must eat three meals a day. They also must schedule several snacks in between. It is important that they never skip a meal. If they do, their blood sugar could get so low that they would pass out. People with diabetes must be careful to eat a certain amount of food. They keep track of it by weighing portions on a simple scale.

A person with diabetes should usually eat plenty of fruits and vegetables, lean meat and fish, whole-grain breads and cereals, and dried beans. Many of these foods release sugar to the body slowly. A diabetic should also limit the amount of fat and cholesterol he or she eats. These have been shown to add to a fatty buildup inside the blood vessels. The buildup could lead to heart disease.

The foods in this kind of diet may sound familiar. Doctors now recommend them for everyone, not just diabetics. What used to be special "dietetic" foods are now sold everywhere and are part of a healthy diet for everyone.

The many kinds of sugar-free drinks and low-fat foods available today give people with diabetes more choices than they used to have. They also make it easier for a diabetic to fit in. For example, there is nothing unusual about someone at a party choosing to drink a sugar-free cola.

For those with diabetes, exercise is an important part of keeping "in balance." Exercise improves the body's blood flow. It helps stop fatty buildup in the blood vessels. It helps the body use foods. It also relieves stress and makes people feel better about themselves.

People with Type I diabetes try to exercise after a meal when their blood sugar is higher. They usually measure their blood sugar both before and after they exercise.

Diabetics are
encouraged to
exercise regu-
larly to help
keep their
blood sugar
levels under
control.

People with Type II diabetes usually
don't have to inject insulin. Controlling
their illness lies in balancing food and
exercise. Their food needs are like those
of Type I diabetics. But there is a difference in the balance they are trying to
keep. Those with Type II diabetes must
be careful to stay away from fatty foods.
They may also have to take non-insulin
medicine prescribed by their doctors.

Scientists know there is a link between
being overweight and getting diabetes.
Research shows that some people with
Type II don't have enough insulin receptors on their cells. These receptors act as
keyholes that allow the insulin to unlock
the doors to the cells. Doctors have discovered that the more fat a person has,
the fewer receptors he or she has. When a
person loses weight, the receptors multi-
ply. Then the insulin can get in and do its

job. That is why it is so important for people with Type II diabetes to control their weight.

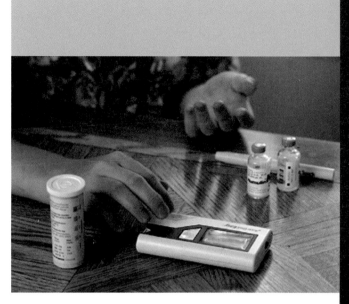

Some people with Type II diabetes take pills to lower their blood sugar. These pills are not insulin. But they help the pancreas produce insulin. They also help the insulin to do its job. Some of these drugs don't mix well with other common medicines, such as cold pills and aspirin. Packages of common medicines often carry a warning that people with diabetes should check with their doctors before taking any. Alcohol doesn't mix well with some drugs that help control blood sugar.

Sometimes even these medicines, a

good diet, and exercise can't control Type II diabetes. In those cases, people with Type II also have to inject themselves with insulin each day.

There is another important factor that helps those with diabetes control the disease: the love and support of families and friends. The support of others helps to reduce stress. Research shows that less stress leads to a lower blood-sugar level. And people who have family and friends who care about them usually want to take good care of themselves.

Chapter 6

Taking Care of Problems

Balancing diet and exercise with insulin or pills isn't always easy. A person may go on an outing and get more exercise than usual. Or a person with diabetes may have a soft drink that he or she believes is sugar-free, only to discover that it isn't. Sometimes we all get into situations—perhaps the car or our regular transportation breaks down—when we can't get to a meal or a snack.

When diet and exercise are off, a person with diabetes often gets high or low blood sugar. Taking too little or too much insulin also spells trouble for a person with diabetes.

Blood Sugar Levels

High blood sugar is called **hyperglycemia**. A person with hyperglycemia may feel thirsty and have to urinate frequently. Hyperglycemia must be treated early. It can become dangerous because it can lead to a coma.

Sometimes a person with Type I diabetes may not inject enough insulin. Without enough insulin, a diabetic's body can't turn sugar into energy. Then the body starts to break down fats to make energy. When fats are broken down, the body produces waste products called **ketones**.

The body tries to get rid of these ketones, or acid wastes, through the urine. But it can't eliminate a large amount of them, and they begin to build up. This condition is called **ketoacidosis**, and it can be fatal. Testing the urine with a strip, like the strips used to test blood, will show the level of ketones in the urine. A person should follow his or her doctor's advice if the urine shows high amounts of ketones.

People suffering ketoacidosis may have a hard time breathing, may vomit, and may become confused. Their breath may smell fruity. If these conditions are not treated, a coma could follow. If you are a diabetic or with a diabetic who shows these symptoms, it is important to get medical help.

Low blood sugar is called **hypoglycemia**. This condition can happen if a person with diabetes eats too little or exercises too much. It can also occur if a person with Type I diabetes takes too much insulin. Hypoglycemia is often called an insulin reaction or insulin shock.

An insulin reaction can happen suddenly. A person may feel dizzy and shaky and begin to sweat. During a serious reaction, a person may pass out. People can usually stop a mild reaction by eating something. A more serious reaction usually means the person needs to take some form of sugar quickly. Table sugar or honey or a few hard candies may help. Some people with diabetes always carry glucose tablets or a tube of glucose gel to stop such reactions.

A person who passes out from insulin shock needs a drug called **glucagon**. It is injected like insulin, and it raises the blood sugar. If you are with someone who has diabetes and he or she passes out, you should quickly get medical help.

Those with diabetes face a special problem when they get common illnesses such as a cold or flu. Their balancing act becomes harder because the illness affects their blood-sugar levels. Feeling upset about something for a long time can have the same effect on blood sugar as an illness. Each diabetic must work together with the doctor to plan what to do when a cold or flu strikes.

A person with diabetes must be prepared. Family and friends should know what to do if the diabetic needs help. People with diabetes can get medical bracelets or necklaces that show they have diabetes. That way, medical workers will know how to help if there is an emergency.

Diabetics who are planning to travel should always take along extra insulin or pills, blood- and urine-testing materials, and an emergency snack. Being prepared and thinking ahead can help a diabetic stay in control of the illness.

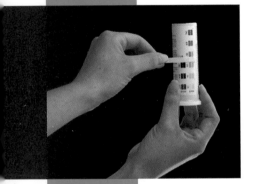

This test strip is coated with a chemical that changes color depending on the level of sugar in the blood. The diabetic can match the color with a scale on the bottle to determine his or her blood sugar level.

Chapter 7

Research into Diabetes

Scientists have been making exciting gains in finding better ways to treat diabetes. They have also been learning more about its causes. They hope someday to discover a prevention and a cure.

Much research aims to find better and easier ways to take insulin. Researchers are also trying to find ways that more closely match what a healthy pancreas does. Some people with diabetes use an insulin pump. This small device is strapped on the body. It delivers insulin through a needle or small tube that is left in place. Companies have been able to make these pumps smaller, more comfortable, and more reliable. But the pumps cost a lot, and not everyone can use them.

Scientists have been trying to make a pumplike device that would be put into the body during surgery. This would do the job of the pancreas. It would keep track of blood sugar and pump insulin as it is needed. Other researchers are trying to make an insulin patch. This would stick to the skin and deliver insulin a little at a time.

Doctors are also excited about an experiment that transplanted into dogs the cells that make insulin. Other projects have involved transplanting the islets of Langerhans. These are the "islands" in the pancreas where the cells that make insulin are found. One researcher put the islets into tiny capsules. The capsules were then put into test animals, where they began to produce insulin. The next step is to try this on humans.

Some diabetics have pancreas transplants. These are most commonly performed in people who also need a kidney transplant. They receive a new pancreas at the same time. Researchers are also testing whether insulin can be taken in a nasal spray.

Testing is also being done to find easier ways to test blood-sugar levels. One device uses infrared light to measure sugar levels. A person shines the light on his or her skin.

The meter shows the sugar level by measuring how much light is absorbed.

Some researchers are trying to find out what causes nerve damage in diabetics. Others report that laser therapy significantly helps in treating eye damage. Some studies focus on trying to prevent kidney problems common to diabetics.

Scientists continue to explore why people with diabetes suffer eye, kidney, and nerve damage. No one has ever found out what causes these problems. Most doctors agree, however, that many of the problems can be slowed or prevented by keeping blood-sugar levels as close to normal as possible.

The cause of diabetes remains a mystery, but ongoing research is encouraging. In a 1993 experiment, scientists were able to prevent mice from getting Type I diabetes. Researchers injected the mice with a molecule to train the mice's immune systems not to attack the pancreas. The early stages of studies in children have shown similar results. More research is needed before doctors know whether the method will work on a wide group of people. Such research holds the promise that someday doctors may be able to prevent and cure diabetes.

Until then, those who have the disease can reduce its effects by taking good care of themselves and by following their treatment plans. Families and friends can help, too, by providing them with love and support.

For Further Reading

Aiello, Barbara. *A Portrait of Me*. Frederick, MD: Twenty-first Century Books, 1989.

Biermann, June, and Barbara Toohey. *The Diabetic's Book: All Your Questions Answered*. Los Angeles: Jeremy Tarcher, 1990.

Diabetes A to Z. Alexandria, VA: American Diabetes Association, 1989.

Diabetes Forecast magazine. Alexandria, VA: American Diabetes Association.

Grilled Cheese at Four O'Clock in the Morning. Alexandria, VA: American Diabetes Association.

Kipnis, Lynne. *You Can't Catch Diabetes from a Friend*. Gainesville, FL: Triad Scientific Publishers, 1979.

Loring, Gloria. *Parenting a Diabetic Child*. Los Angeles: Lowell House, 1991.

Tiger, Steven. *Diabetes*. New York: J. Messner, 1987.

For More Information

American Diabetes Association
1660 Duke Street
Alexandria, VA 22314
1-800-ADA-DISC
(Check the phone book for your local
    chapter.)

Juvenile Diabetes Foundation International
432 Park Avenue South
New York, NY 10016-8103
1-800-223-1138

National Diabetes Information Clearinghouse
Box NDIC
Bethesda, MD 20892
301-468-2162

Glossary

autoimmune Describing a condition in which the body mistakes its own cells for harmful germs and destroys the cells. Type I diabetes is an autoimmune disease because the body destroys the cells in the pancreas that make insulin.

blood sugar The amount of sugar in a person's blood. Problems occur if the blood contains too much or too little sugar.

coma The condition in which someone is deeply unconscious.

diabetes mellitus A disease that prevents the body from using and storing sugar for energy. It happens when the body doesn't have enough insulin or when the body can't use its insulin.

dialysis A treatment in which a machine removes waste from a person's blood after his or her kidneys have failed.

glucagon A drug that is injected into a diabetic who has passed out from insulin shock. Glucagon raises the blood sugar.

glucose A simple sugar that is the body's main source of energy.

hormone A chemical that brings a message from one part of the body to another. The message tells the body what to do.

hyperglycemia The condition in which there is too much sugar in the blood. It is also called high blood sugar.

hypoglycemia A condition in which there is not enough sugar in the blood. It is also called low blood sugar.

insulin A hormone that allows the body's cells to use the food we eat. It is made by the beta cells in the pancreas.

islets of Langerhans Clusters of cells in the pancreas where the beta cells are located.

ketoacidosis A condition that occurs when the body goes a long time without enough insulin. Ketoacidosis can lead to coma and death. This condition can happen in Type I diabetes.

ketones Acids that form in the blood. They occur when the body uses fat to make energy. Ketones show up in the urine, and if they build up, ketoacidosis occurs.

kidneys A pair of organs located below and behind the stomach that filter wastes from our bodies.

pancreas A gland located behind the stomach. One of its jobs is to make insulin.

syringe A device for giving insulin shots. It is often called a needle.

Index